FAN CLUB

I Love ROBERT PATTINSON

Kat Miller

WINDMILL
BOOKS

New York

For Morgan Downer

Published in 2011 by Windmill Books, LLC
303 Park Avenue South, Suite # 1280, New York, NY 10010-3657

Copyright © 2011 by Windmill Books, LLC

CREDITS:
Editor: Jennifer Way
Book Design: Erica Clendening and Greg Tucker
Photo Research: Ashley Burrell

Photo Credits: Cover, p. 22 Steve Granitz/WireImage/Getty Images; p. 4 Frazer Harrison/ Getty Images; pp. 5, 10 Franco Origlia/Getty Images; p. 6 Daniele Venturelli/WireImage/ Getty Images; pp. 7, 13, 14, 15 (left), 16, 18 (top), 18–19 (bottom) Shutterstock.com; pp. 8–9 Dave M. Benett/Getty Images; p. 11 Jeffrey Mayer/WireImage/Getty Images; p. 12 Kevin Winter/Getty Images; p. 15 (top) James Devaney/WireImages/Getty Images; pp. 16–17 Jon Kopaloff/FilmMagic/Getty Images; p. 19 (top) Jun Sato/WireImage/Getty Images; pp. 20–21 Soul Brother/FilmMagic/Getty Images.

Library of Congress Cataloging-in-Publication Data

Miller, Kat.
  I love Robert Pattinson / by Kat Miller.
     p. cm. — (Fan club)
  Includes index.
  ISBN 978-1-61533-057-7 (library binding) — ISBN 978-1-61533-058-4 (pbk.) — ISBN 978-1-61533-059-1 (6-pack)
  1. Pattinson, Robert, 1986—Juvenile literature. 2. Motion picture actors and actresses Juvenile literature—Great Britain—Biography I. Title.
  PN2598.P36M55 2011
  792.0'28092—dc22
  [B]
                                    2010007629

Manufactured in the United States of America

For more great fiction and nonfiction, go to windmillbooks.com.

CPSIA Compliance Information: Batch #S10W: For further information contact Windmill Books, New York, New York at 1-866-478-0556.

Contents

Meet Robert Pattinson

Robert Pattinson is one of today's most popular movie stars. He is often known by his nickname, Rob. Robert is best known for playing Edward Cullen in the Twilight movies. His **performance** as Edward has won him lots of fans. They are proud to say that they are on "Team Edward."

Robert Pattinson, seen here, has a huge number of fans. Many of his fans were won over by his good looks.

4

Robert has even won **awards** for his performance. In 2009, he won several MTV Movie Awards. He has won several Teen Choice Awards, too.

Here is Robert on the *New Moon* movie set in Italy.

5

Robert Thomas Pattinson was born in London, England, on May 13, 1986. His parents are Richard and Clare Pattinson. Robert's father sold **vintage** cars. His mother worked for a **modeling agency**. Robert has two older sisters, named Elizabeth and Victoria.

His time as a model prepared Robert for having his picture taken a lot when he became a big movie star.

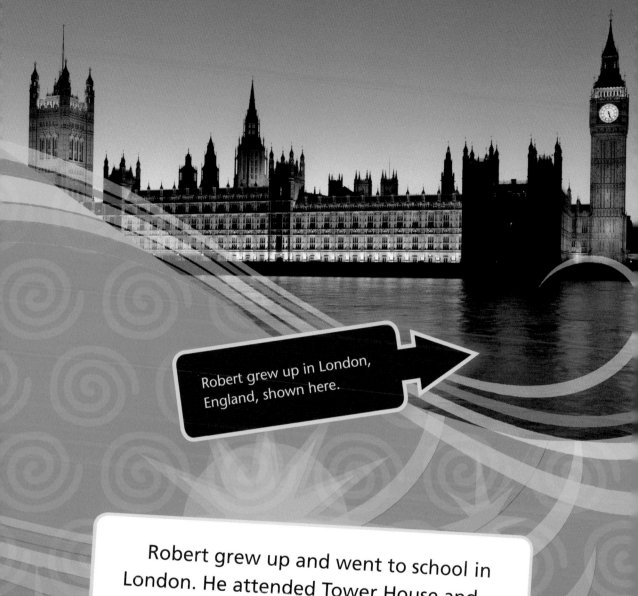

Robert grew up in London, England, shown here.

Robert grew up and went to school in London. He attended Tower House and Harrodian School. There, Robert took part in school plays. He also was a model for several years.

Cedric Diggory

Stanislav Ianevski

Clémence Poésy

Rupert Grint

In 2004, Robert appeared in a TV movie called *Ring of the Nibelungs*. Later that year, he won the part of Cedric Diggory in the movie *Harry Potter and the Goblet of Fire*. It was part of a popular **series** of movies about a young wizard named Harry Potter.

In *Harry Potter and the Goblet of Fire*, Robert (far right) got to work with great co-stars.

8

Emma
Watson

Daniel
Radcliffe

Katie
Leung

Robert
Pattinson

9

Edward Cullen

This picture of Robert and Kristen is from a photo shoot for the *New Moon* movie poster.

In December 2007, Robert was **cast** as the **vampire** Edward Cullen in the movie *Twilight*. The movie was based on the first in a series of books by Stephenie Meyer. They are about a girl named Bella Swan who falls in love with Edward Cullen.

Kristen Stewart plays Edward's true love Bella Swan in the Twilight movies. Kristen (right) and Robert (left) got along well.

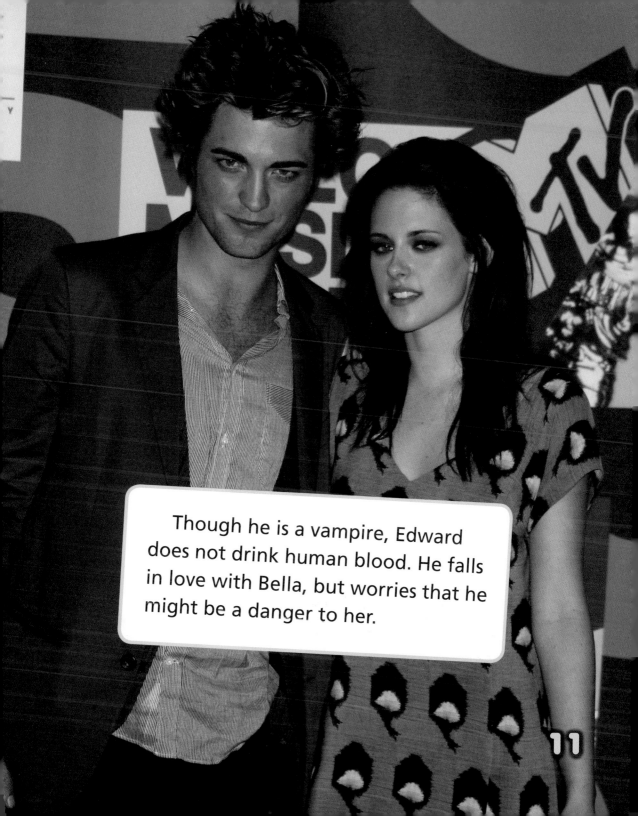

Though he is a vampire, Edward does not drink human blood. He falls in love with Bella, but worries that he might be a danger to her.

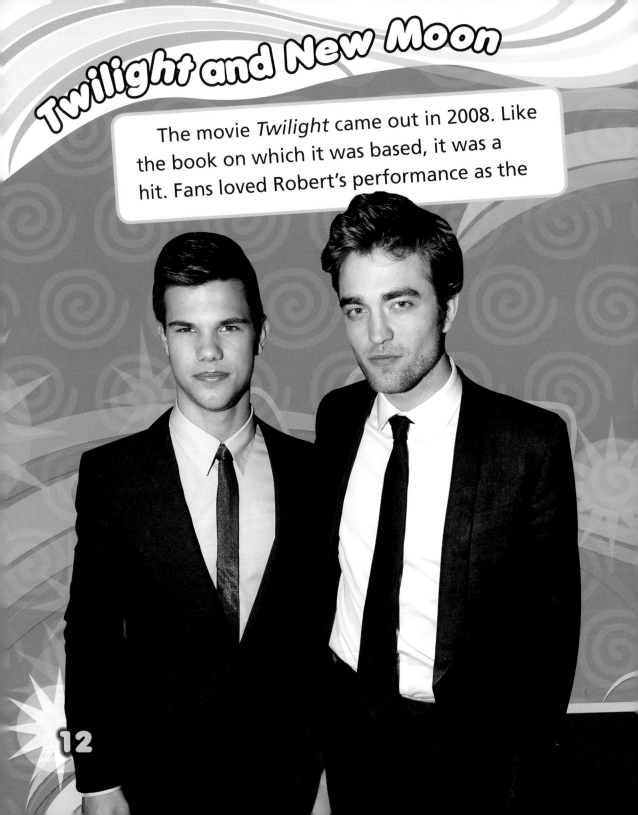

Twilight and New Moon

The movie *Twilight* came out in 2008. Like the book on which it was based, it was a hit. Fans loved Robert's performance as the

The Twilight series is set in Washington. This part of the United States is known for having lots of dark, cloudy days. That's a good thing if you are a vampire!

vampire Edward. They were moved by the love story between Bella and Edward.

In 2009, Robert starred in *The Twilight Saga: New Moon*, the second movie in the Twilight series. In it, Edward leaves Bella to try to keep her safe. By the movie's end, he admits that he really loves her.

In *The Twilight Saga: New Moon*, both Edward and the werewolf Jacob Black are in love with Bella. Jacob is played by Taylor Lautner (left). Here are Taylor and Robert in 2009.

Emilie de Ravin starred in *Remember Me* with Robert.

Though he is best known for playing Edward Cullen, Robert has played several different characters in the past few years. He was in a comedy called *How to Be* in 2008. That same year, he played the Spanish artist Salvador Dalí in the movie *Little Ashes*.

Here is Robert in New York City at the opening of *Remember Me*.

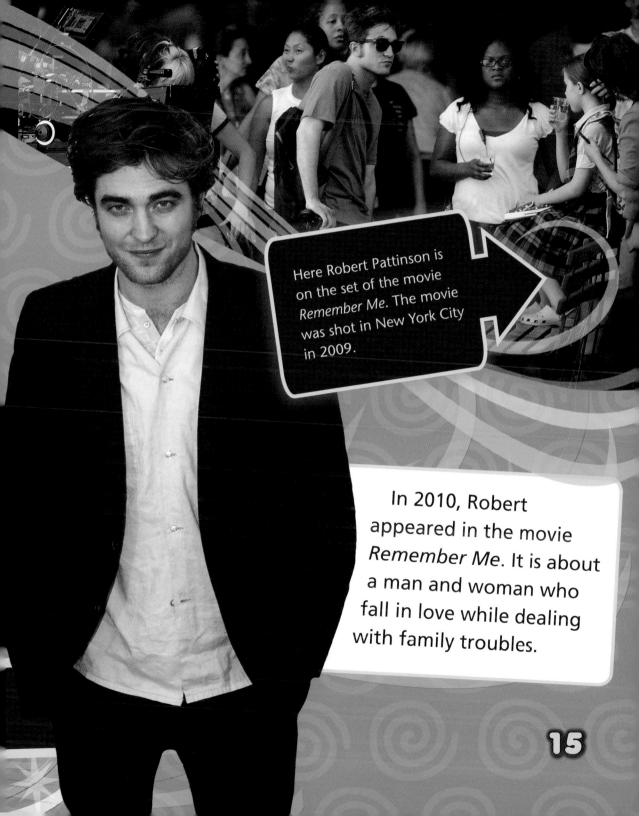

Here Robert Pattinson is on the set of the movie *Remember Me*. The movie was shot in New York City in 2009.

In 2010, Robert appeared in the movie *Remember Me*. It is about a man and woman who fall in love while dealing with family troubles.

Making Music

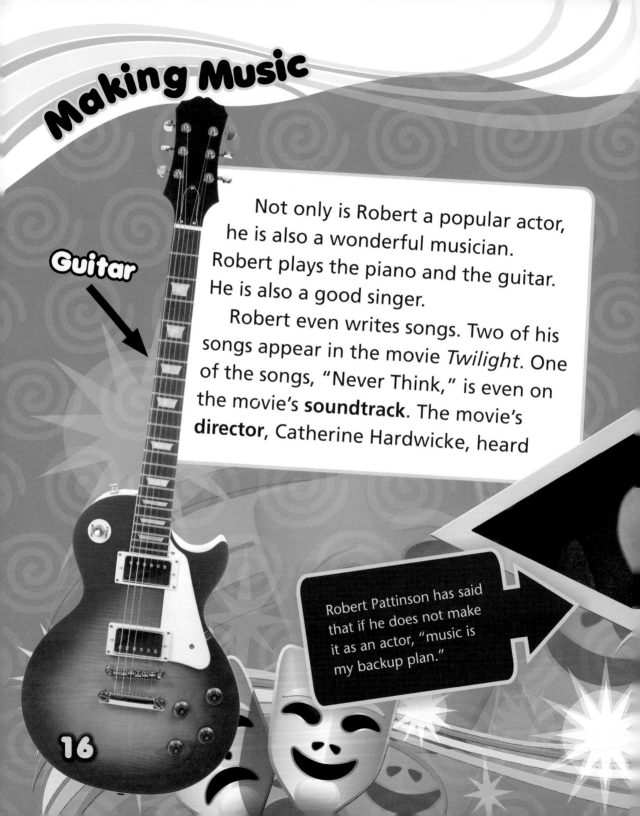

Guitar

Not only is Robert a popular actor, he is also a wonderful musician. Robert plays the piano and the guitar. He is also a good singer.

Robert even writes songs. Two of his songs appear in the movie *Twilight*. One of the songs, "Never Think," is even on the movie's **soundtrack**. The movie's **director**, Catherine Hardwicke, heard

Robert Pattinson has said that if he does not make it as an actor, "music is my backup plan."

his songs and thought they were so good she decided to use them. Robert was surprised, but happy.

Robert and His Fans

Robert Pattinson has some of the world's most enthusiastic fans. His fans want to know what is going on in Robert's life. They have set up many Web sites on which to post news and pictures of him.

Robert gets to go around the world to promote, or talk to people about, his movies. Here he is in 2009 at a film festival in Cannes, France.

Here, Robert Pattinson is meeting with fans at the premiere, or opening, of *Twilight* in Los Angeles, California, in November 2008.

When Robert appears in public, fans often rush up to him. Some fans want to have their picture taken with him. Others are just filled with wonder to see their favorite star in person.

Sometimes Robert's female fans rush up to him to meet him.

Looking Ahead

In summer 2010, the third Twilight movie came out. It was called *The Twilight Saga: Eclipse*. Once again, Robert starred in it. There are also plans to make a movie of *Breaking Dawn*, the fourth book in the Twilight series. Robert will appear again as Edward Cullen. The book is so long that it might become two movies.

Robert Pattinson is one of the biggest stars today. He is likely to be around for many years to come.

In just a few years, Robert has become a huge star. Who knows what will come next?

Just Like Me!

1 Robert Pattinson has a pet dog named Patty. Patty is a West Highland White Terrier.

2 Like many youngest children, Robert sometimes got bossed around as a kid.

3 One of Robert's favorite foods is spaghetti and meatballs.

4 Robert reads a lot. He has said that reading books is one of his favorite things to do.

5 Robert likes watching other actors' work. Jack Nicholson is one of his favorite actors.

Glossary

awards (uh-WORDS) Special honors given to someone.

cast (KAST) Picked to play a part.

director (dih-REK-ter) The person who tells movie or play actors what to do.

modeling agency (MAH-duhl-ling AY-jen-see) A business that hires people to show off clothes.

performance (per-FOR-mens) The playing of a character.

series (SIR-eez) A group of similar things that come one after another.

soundtrack (SOWND-trak) A group of songs from a movie or TV show.

vampire (VAM-py-er) A dead person from stories and folktales who sucks the blood of living people.

vintage (VIN-tij) Old and valuable.

Index

Read More

Rusher, Josie. *Robert Pattinson: True Love Never Dies*. London: Orion Publishing Group, 2009.

Vaz, Mark Cotta. *Twilight: The Complete Illustrated Movie Companion*. New York: Little, Brown, 2008.

Williams, Mel. *Robert Pattinson: Fated for Fame*. New York: Simon & Schuster, 2009.

Web Sites

For Web resources related to the subject of this book, go to: www.windmillbooks.com/weblinks and select this book's title.